More Cat Tales

Starring Hodge

Produced by Philip Lief

A WALLABY BOOK
Published by Simon & Schuster
NEW YORK

SEVERAL HUMAN FRIENDS PROVIDED INVALUABLE ASSISTANCE IN THE PREPARATION OF THIS BOOK. KEN LAWLESS PERFORMED THE HERCULEAN TASK OF TRANSLATING FELINE PROFUNDITY INTO ORDINARY HUMAN SPEECH; NICK DE CANDIA BROUGHT AN EXPERT EYE AND TRUE PROFESSIONALISM TO HIS WORK AS MY PERSONAL PHOTOGRAPHER; LESLIE WHEELER AND RENA BONNÉ SUPPLIED GOOD EDITORIAL JUDGMENT; AND ILONA T. SHERRATT DID THE BEAUTIFUL WRITING. I AM ALSO DEEPLY GRATEFUL TO THE SCHENECTADY MUSEUM FOR THE USE OF ITS MARVELOUS FACILITIES; AND TO THE A.S.P.C.A. FOR PROVIDING A WARM AND CARING ENVIRONMENT DURING A TRANSITION PERIOD IN MY LIFE.

PUBLISHED BY WALLABY BOOKS
A SIMON & SCHUSTER DIVISION OF GULF & WESTERN CORPORATION

SIMON & SCHUSTER BUILDING
1230 AVENUE OF THE AMERICAS
NEW YORK, NEW YORK 10020

WALLABY AND COLOPHON ARE REGISTERED TRADEMARKS OF SIMON & SCHUSTER

FIRST WALLABY BOOKS PRINTING NOVEMBER, 1981
MANUFACTURED IN THE UNITED STATES OF AMERICA

10 9 8 7 6 5 4 3 2 1

ISBN 0-671-43761-5

SOUTHFIELD, MASS.

A Few Words From Hodge

FOR YEARS NOW, PUBLISHERS HAVE BEEN HOUNDING ME TO WRITE MY MEMOIRS. THEIR MOTIVES WERE FRANKLY MERCENARY. THEY REASONED THAT IF HUMANKIND WAS FASCINATED BY THE IMAGINARY ANTICS OF CARTOON CATS, THE TRUE STORY OF A REAL CAT WOULD BE A BLOCKBUSTER. UNCONVINCED THAT HUMANKIND DESERVED THE WIT AND WISDOM OF A REAL CAT, I DEVOTED MY FIERCE FELINE ENERGIES TO OTHER PURSUITS, CHIEFLY TO MY SUCCESS-FUL CAREER AS A WRITER OF SONGS IN THE BEST TRADITION OF TIN PAN ALLEY AND NASHVILLE, AND TO MY SOLITARY QUEST FOR THE PURR-FECT NAP.

IF I HAVE RELENTED, IT IS PRIMARILY FROM A SENSE OF NOBLESSE OBLIGE. THE NATURAL SUPERIORITY OF CATS PLACES A GRAVE RESPONSIBILITY UPON US TO PUT THAT ADVANTAGE TO GOOD USE. HUMANKIND IS NOT DOING TOO WELL ON ITS OWN. IT IS HIGH TIME FOR FELIS DOMESTICA TO TAKE PITY ON POOR HAPLESS HOMO SAPIENS. THIS IS THE MOMENT FOR HODGE TO TELL HER OWN STORY IN HER OWN WORDS.

MY QUEST FOR THE PURR-FECT NAP HAS BEEN GENERALLY MISUNDERSTOOD. IT IS PROMPTED BY THE PUREST OF MOTIVES AND BY THE HIGHEST IDEALS. MY QUEST FOR THE PURR-FECT NAP IS AS NOBLE AS LANCELOT'S QUEST FOR THE HOLY GRAIL. NOT FOR HODGE THE BANAL COMFORTS OF AN ORDINARY CAT NAP, OR THE EVERYDAY PLEASURES OF A SNOOZE IN THE NOONDAY SUN. TO ME, THE NAP IS A CEREMONIAL OCCASION, A RITUAL WITH SPIRITUAL OVERTONES. A CAT CAN ENJOY MORE SHEER SENSUAL PLEASURE FROM A NAP THAN PEOPLE ENJOY FROM...JUST ABOUT ANYTHING YOU WOULD CARE TO NAME.

SIMILARLY, MY FONDNESS FOR MEAT HAS BEEN DISTORTED BY THE SEN-SATIONALIST MEDIA. IT IS TRUE THAT I COMMONLY DISDAIN KIBBLE, BUT HOW MANY PEOPLE CAN YOU NAME WHO PREFER CORN FLAKES TO PRIME RIBS? AS A CAT, I AM A CONNOISSEUR, NATURE'S QUINTESSENTIAL GOURMET. MY TASTES RUN TO BEEF BOURGUINONNE, TO BABY LAMB CHOPS, TO PATÉ DE FOIE GRAS, THOUGH I HAVE BEEN KNOWN TO PILFER A PEPPERONI FROM A PIZZA. FOR THIS PASSION FOR PROTEIN, I HAVE BEEN CALLED A NOTORIOUS CARNIVORE. I AM NOT ASHAMED TO ADMIT AS MUCH; HODGE WAS NOT BORN TO SHAME.

I AM CHEERFULLY TOLERANT OF MY FELLOW CREATURES, EVEN SHARING MY QUARTERS WITH A CANINE NAMED ANGUS MACDOGGAL. NO ONE WOULD ACCUSE ANGUS OF BEING QUICK-WITTED, SINCE QUICK-WITTED CREATURES NEVER CHASE CARS. BUT HE DOES HAVE CERTAIN REDEEMING QUALITIES: HE'S LOYAL, GOOD-NATURED, AND BEST OF ALL, HE ADORES MY SONGS. AT HIS URGING, I HAVE INCLUDED A SAMPLING OF MY HIT TUNES LIKE "THE LITTERED LITTERBOX BLUES" IN THE PRESENT VOLUME.

IT HAS NOT BEEN AN EASY TASK TO PREPARE THIS BOOK. THE PUBLISHERS WANTED A DOCUMENTARY FLAVOR. "TRY TO LOOK ORDINARY," THEY SAID. BUT I AM A <u>CAT</u>, AND A CAT CAN NO MORE LOOK ORDINARY FOR A CAMERA THAN GARBO COULD LOOK DRAB FOR ONE. WHAT YOU SEE HERE IS A FAITHFUL RECORD OF THE DAYS AND WAYS OF HODGE.

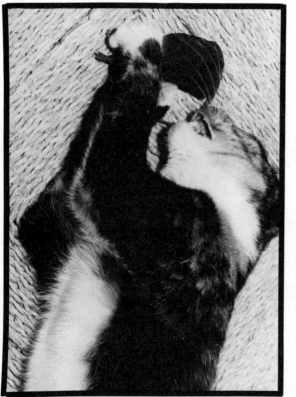
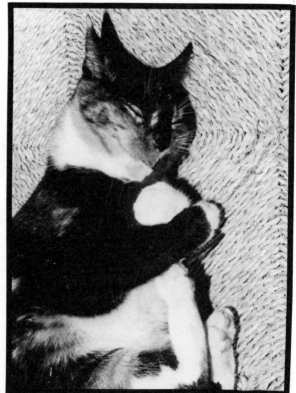

THE MERE SIGHT OF MILK IS SUPPOSED TO MAKE A CAT PURR.

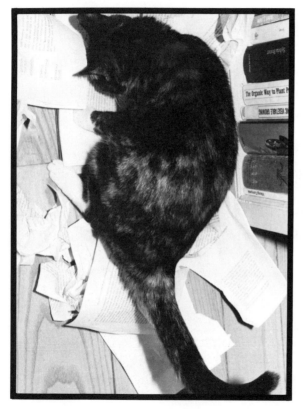

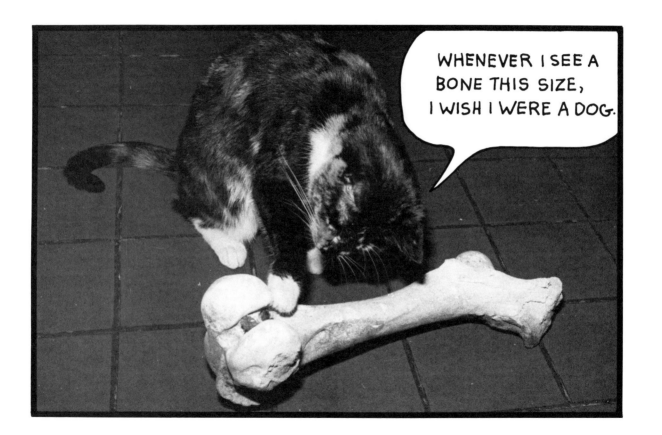

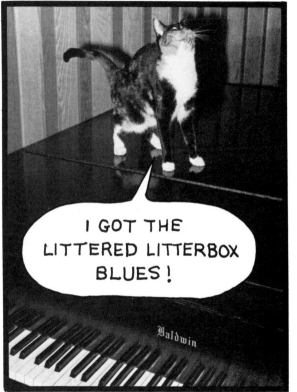

THE PURR-FECT NAP
HAS THUS FAR ELUDED ME.

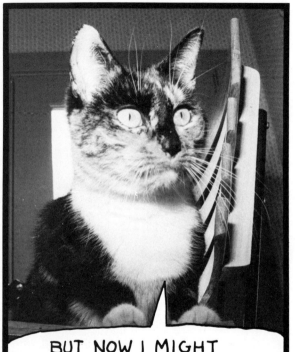

BUT NOW I MIGHT
ACHIEVE PERFECTION.